A Strong Tower

BY M.D. MAGRUDER-KRINOCK

A Strong Tower

Editor: Camille Mitchell

ISBN-13: 9780615674506
ISBN-10: 061567450X

Ministry Information:
Lifeline Outreach Int'l

1.888.505.5393
www.mariakrinock.com
www.lifelineoutreach.com

Friend us on Facebook
http://facebook.com/maria.magruder

Publisher: WebsitesGlobal.com Publishing

Rev. 021114

Special Acknowledgement

Special "Thanks" to my father and mother in the faith:

Apostles Doctors
Christian & Robin Harfouche

Thank you for your love, support and teaching of the Word and Spirit of God.

And Thank you for pioneering the best bible school on the planet -

International Miracle Institute

WWW.IMILIVE.ORG

TABLE OF CONTENTS

Chapter One

The UFC Christian

There are two types of Christians, one who goes to church every Sunday and leaves the way they came and the other who changes and transforms. The first one is the Christian whom we would call a "roller coaster" Christian because they go up and down in their walk with Christ. This is the Christian who struggles with their joy, and with every circumstance that opposes them in life and life is quite the drama for them. This is the Christian who you do not want to ask, "How's it going?" because you know that it's going to be a long drama of their whole week and you will be stuck listening to doubt and unbelief for the next hour! The second type of Christian is the one that's consistently full of the joy of the Lord and is walking in victory. I like to call this Christian the UFC or the Ultimate Fighting Christian. They do not know the meaning of the words: quit, failure, losing, defeat, or decrease. They do know the words, victory, overcome, winning, gaining, increase, and forward. This is the Christian who understands it takes more than just going to church every Sunday. This is the Christian who understands that even though the battle is already won that there is still an opponent out there who opposes the call of God and knows there must be training to run the race with endurance.

What is the difference between the Christian who doesn't want to change and the UFC (Ultimate Fighting Christian)? One Christian has understanding and revelation of the authority that Christ has given them through the way of the cross and the other does not. The Christian who has received a revelation of their authority has allowed the Word of God to change and transform them. This Christian is NOT a victim in their circumstances, but instead is in dominion. This is the Christian who, when they go to church, goes with the expectation of leaving at a higher level than when they came. They came to hear the word, believe the word and apply the word. It doesn't matter what comes their way, they maintain joy and peace, and they are not moved. They have the victory even though the circumstance is attempting to state otherwise.

If you are reading this book, then I am confident you are one of the Ultimate Fighting Christians as you would not be reading this book if you were not hungry for more of God! What UFC fighter goes into the ring with no training and conditioning? In the next few chapters we will make it clear to you, through the Word of God, and will also help you to understand and gain revelation of this authority that belongs to you, the Believer! If you have a good understanding of authority already, the Lord will take you to another level in your understanding. We never approach God as "I have heard that before." Instead, we approach God with expectation of receiving and growing in Him. There is no limit to our growth in God!

Jesus said in *Matthew 28:18, "All authority has been given unto me in Heaven and on earth."* And in *John 16:15 NKJV* we find Jesus saying: "*All things that the Father has are Mine.* Therefore I said that He will take of Mine and declare it to you." Therefore all the authority that Jesus has been given in heaven and on earth has been given to those who are in Christ Jesus, to those who are sons and daughters of God. Unfortunately, many sons and daughters of God are living and breathing on this earth not knowing or understanding their authority, which has been freely given to them. They are therefore walking at a sub-standard level instead of what has already been provided. It is of the utmost importance for us as Believers to take the time to study and look at what Christ has purchased for us on the cross concerning authority.

The purpose of authority is to make God's will and resources available to you so that you can receive the same results that Jesus does. Authority provides the vehicle to access God's resources and His will. If we find ourselves failing to cash in on God's resources the problem is not the lack of God's willingness to do what He said He would, the problem is our slackness in exercising the authority that has been given to us. This is why we must understand and learn how to walk in our authority every day. When we understand what God has given us with authority, we will understand that it is our right to live the high call of God, that it is our right to decree and partake of all of God's promises.

Chapter Two

What Is Authority?

Authority can be found all the way back to the beginning of the Book! We find in Genesis that God gave dominion to mankind in the garden. We see this in *Genesis 1:28 NLT "Then God blessed them and said, "Be fruitful and multiply. Fill the earth and govern it. Reign over the fish in the sea, the birds in the sky, and all the animals that scurry along the ground."* Right from the beginning God had intended for mankind to have rulership and govern things on this earth. It has always been God's plan for us to be living and walking in the realm of kings and priests. We lost that dominion and authority during "the fall." When Adam and Eve made that decision of disobedience, they forfeited mankind's authority and sin then was granted liberty and given an entrance into the earth. When Adam and Eve fell they were instantly separated from God.

We see this in Genesis 2:17 NKJV *"but of the tree of the knowledge of good and evil you shall not eat, for in the day that you eat of it you shall surely die."* We know that Adam and Eve didn't "die" instantly, but they were instantly separated from God. When we are separated from God we are separated from the life of God and we are no longer connected to Him. Therefore, the death process of aging and decline begins. Whereas before sin entered the earth there was no aging or declining in their physical bodies. Death is to be *"separated from God"* How is this related to authority? I'm glad you asked! Authority as we saw earlier is *GIVEN*. Remember? *Matthew 18:18 NKJV - said, "All authority has been given unto me in Heaven and on earth."* Jesus even received His authority by it being *given* to Him. The Father GAVE Him all authority in Heaven and *on earth*. This means in order for authority to work and be effective there must be a connection - a connection to a higher realm. A connection that is greater and that carries the life of God, power and authority.

Authority and dominion were GIVEN to Adam and Eve. Through dis-obedience death came in, and separated them from God.

"Therefore, just as through one man sin entered the world and death through sin, and thus death spread to all men, because all sinned." Romans 5:12 NKJV

Adam and Eve lost the connection of authority at that point, and for all mankind. No longer could they command the beast of the field what to do. No longer would the earth cooperate with them when they spoke to it. Now they had to toil and work the land, and the land was non-responsive to the voice and authority of Adam and Eve because there was now no connection between them and God, as they had become separated. Authority was lost at that point, and instead of ruling in authority, they were now sub-serviant and under the rulership of the devil. It is important to understand from what we see and learn how sin entered the earth and that it was through "dis-obedience" to God's commands and instructions.

"For if by one man's offense death reigned through the one, much more those who receive abundance of grace and of the gift of righteousness will reign in life through the One, Jesus Christ."
Romans 5:17 NKJV

We see from the above scripture that death and sin reign through disobedience. When we hear the word offense our mind immediately goes to "I'm offended" or being offended by someone's action.

Offense in the Greek means "to fall or a lapse/ deviation from Truth and uprightness." The devil can only work through our disobedience by us falling away from Truth or Gods Word. Unbelief is disobedience because it is falling away from the Truth. The only power the devil has is a big mouth. All the devil has are words. If one listens and acts on those words that is where he is given any sort of power at all. We also see from the scripture above that if sin can rule and reign through dis-obedience how much more those, who have been given the gift of salvation through Jesus Christ and have become a new creation, can rule and reign in this life!

When Jesus went to the cross, died and rose again, He took possession of the keys that the devil had obtained deceitfully from mankind and brought them back for us! No longer do we have to live substandardly! We once again have the authority that God originally had intended for us in the garden.

What does authority really mean? In the Greek it means "*exousia.*" Here are just a few of the mean-ings in the Greek:

1. power of choice

2. the power of authority (influence) and of right (privilege)

3. the power of rule or government (the power of him whose will and commands must be submitted to by others and obeyed)

4. the power over judicial decisions

5. authority to manage domestic affairs

6. a ruler, a human magistrate

Starting with just definition one, we have the power of choice! The word of God says we have the choice to choose life or death.

"I call heaven and earth as witnesses today against you, that I have set before you life and death, blessing and cursing; therefore choose life, that both you and your decendants may live;"
Dueteronmy 30:19 NKJV

God has given us choice. We choose how we live. This means we choose what we allow and don't allow in life. We have the opportunity to choose either blessing or cursing each and every day. If we choose blessing and life, then we will live a life that is full of God's goodness beyond what we can think or imagine. Blessing and cursing both come from the same place, our mouth! One of the keys in learning and operating in your authority is to monitor what is coming out of your mouth. The mouth is the gateway to either life or death. Our own mouth can be our greatest friend or our worst enemy. We have the power to speak things into existence, whether good or negative. If you speak that you are sick then you have just given sickness, by YOUR authority, the right and permission to reside in your body. Jesus said you can have in your life whatever you say.

"For assuredly, I say to you, whoever says to this mountain, 'Be removed and be cast into the sea,' and does not doubt in his heart, but believes that those things he says will be done, he will have whatever he says."
Mark 11:23 NKJV

We see from the above scripture that we have the power to speak to "things." If we can speak things to be removed, surely we can speak them to "be." Just as God said, "Let there be!" The good news is we don't have to say, "we are sick." Instead, we can say, "I am healed by the stripes Jesus paid according to Isaiah 53." We can remove any mountain in our life just by what we allow to come out of our mouth. This is a great blessing for the Christian, as long as we choose life to come out of our mouth. It is also a great responsibility, because if we do not choose life, then the results will be the things of this natural world and sin.

Bringing our attention to definitions two and three of exousia, which is the influence of the right and privilege and the power to rule. It is our right and privilege to rule and have things submit to us. It is our right to exercise our authority and have "things" obey us. We are citizens of God's kingdom and that gives us the right to have what God has promised us in His Word, whether it be divine health and healing, prosperity or even deliverance from our enemies. It is our given right to not have any weapon prosper that is formed against us. It is our right to lay hands on someone with an incurable disease and see them recover. It is our right to cast out devils. If there is a devil messing with your finances, your stuff or your physical body, you have the right to cast that thing out!

As we continue to discover what authority means, we find in the standard Webster's dictionary that authority means:

1. The power to determine, adjudicate, settle issues or disputes; jurisdiction, the right to control, command or determine.

2. A power or right delegated or given; authoriza-

tion; one who has the power to grant permission.

3.   Persons having the legal power to make and enforce the law; government.

To help us understand God's authority, let's look at some natural analogies. On this earth we have "authorities." We have law enforcement, we have judges in the judicial systems, we have courts that make decisions to decide what is right and wrong, and to sentence if need be. We have military that help to keep the peace of our nations. All these authorities are within our government to help keep things in order and by law.

You will find that a law enforcement officer has a badge. What does that badge state? It is stating that that officer has "authority" and the power to back up that authority. He or she has authority to write tickets and fine those who are breaking the law. That officer has the power to "command." If a person decides to not obey the officers commands then the officer has the power to back up their commands by arresting or if need be use a gun to enforce the law and make an arrest.

It is the same in God's kingdom. He has given us the right to settle issues, and the legal power to enforce commands. As in the standard dictionary above in definition #2 we have been given the right and authorization to even grant permission. We have been given the right to grant "things" permission in our lives. If there is something in your life good or bad it's there by permission. We are priests and kings in Gods kingdom. We have the right to accept or reject what is being presented to us. Just as in the natural, a judge in a court system has the right to "judge" a case legal or illegal. Just as a law enforcement officer wears a badge that states authority, so a judge wears a robe that states they have the authority to judge the case according to the law set in place. The judge has the right and authority to settle disputes and issues. When a judge makes a decision on a case and declares "guilty or "not guilty" it's followed up by action. Either that person is set free with a "not guilty" verdict or sentenced if "guilty." The judge has the power to sentence and enforce that sentence to those who have broken the law. With the authority we have been given by Christ, we in our lives can judge the things in this earth and in heaven. Just as the judge judges a case by the laws set in place, we judge by the law of God's Word that has been settled in Heaven. If things in your life are not lining up with God's promises and they are "law" breakers then we have the right to judge those things. Law breakers are anything that is not lining up with the promises of God's Word. You have the right to be walking in divine health. If a physical symptom comes on you of sickness of any kind that thing is breaking the law of God. The word says "...and nothing by any means shall hurt them." Therefore, that sickness is breaking the law and you have the right to judge, and sentence that thing and cast it off!

Chapter Three

Levels of Authority

There are different levels of authority on this earth. For example, the President of the United States has more authority than a state representative. The Chief of Police has more authority than a regular street officer. The employer has more authority than the employee. But the employee and the state representative have a realm of influence of their authority that has been given to them to oversee. The employer expects that employee is to watch over the area that has been assigned to them and take care of any issues that may arise. The state representative may not have jurisdiction over the whole country as the President does, but they do have jurisdiction over the state they have been assigned. The regular law enforcement officer has been given a jurisdiction over an area of the city. This is their realm of authority and where they can exercise their authority. An officer may have authority in one city, but has not been granted authority in another. Their authority will only work in the city or precinct given. If an officer were to try to exercise their authority in a precinct that was not assigned to them or given to them, their authority would not work and their judgments or arrests would not stand in court. Authority is GIVEN and assigned.

Just as in the natural realm, the spirit realm is the same. Authority is given. There are levels of authority.

"And He Himself gave some to be apostles, some prophets, some evangelists and some pastors and teachers."
Ephesians 4:12 NKJV

Here in Ephesians you see again that authority is *given,* and there are ranks. An apostle has a different jurisdiction than a pastor or teacher, yet they are all ministry gifts to help perfect and equip the saints for the work of the ministry. Therefore the saint, the Believer, has also been given authority and a jurisdiction of rule and reign. Whereas a five-fold gift can have regional and global authority, a Believer has authority over their region of life. This includes their workplace, their family, their neighborhood, their city, and wherever their feet treads. It also includes their bodies, soul and spirit! We have rule and reign over our bodies, over our mind will and emotions, as well as our human spirit. Together, as the body of Christ, we have jurisdiction and rule over the whole planet! Jesus did not withhold authority from the Believer. The same authority to heal the sick and cast out devils belongs to the Believer just as it does the five-fold gifts.

> **"Behold, I give you the authority to trample on serpents and scorpions,and over all the power of the enemy, and nothing shall by any means hurt you."**
> **Luke 10:19 NKJV**

This authority given is not just for the five-fold but for everyone who will believe.

Chapter Four

Enforcing Authority

Why do we see many Christian's authority not working? Or maybe there is an area in your life where authority isn't working. Just because authority has been given to the Believer does not mean the Believer is exercising their authority. Sometimes it is not that one is not exercising their authority but, that they are not enforcing their authority. The devil always resists. It's our job to enforce. It is a very sad thing to see a Believer with all authority and yet they are still being pushed around by forces that oppose the Word of God in their life. It would be like a law enforcement officer watching a person being mugged and robbed on the street and doing nothing. The officer has the authority, the right, the privilege and the power to arrest that criminal yet no authority is being exercised or enforced and therefore the robber gets away with the goods and leaves the person violated and stripped. That is what happens to us when we do not exercise and enforce our authority! The devil always comes to steal, kill and destroy. Whether he comes in life's circumstances or an actual spiritual attack he will not respect authority if you do not exercise it. The devil is a law breaker. This is why authority is needed here on earth.

Authority must carry with it the <u>POWER</u> to back it up. In Luke 10:19 we see authority and power given. Jesus gave us the authority to trample over the serpent and the scorpions and over all the power of the enemy. To "trample" means to CRUSH. We are all most certainly called to CRUSH anything that is opposing the Word of God manifesting in our life. This is the miracle working power of God.

"One day Jesus called together his twelve disciples and gave them power and authority to cast out ALL demons and to heal ALL diseases."
Luke 9:1-2 NLT

The word "power" here in the Greek is "dynamis." In Strong's dictionary dynamis means:

1. Inherent power, power residing in a thing by virtue of its nature

2. Power for performing miracles
3. The power and influence which belong to riches and wealth.
4. Power consisting in or resting upon armies, forces

There is so much in this definition of dynamis, that you should be jumping up and down just reading it!

It is important to understand that in *Luke 9:1-2* that He gave us "authority and power." They work together. If you don't know that you have power, then your authority will not work. This is why it is important for us to take some time to cover dynamis or the miracle working power of God.

Let's just start with the first definition "inherent power, residing" – residing as the miracle working power of God is living and abiding in you! According to Ephesians there is a dynamis power that works in us:

"Now to Him who is able to do exceedingly abundantly above all that we ask or think, according to the power that works in us."
Ephesians 3:20

This dynamis has targeted your house! You are the house of God! Glory! 1st Corinthians 3:16 NKJV reports, "Do you not know that you are the temple of God and that the Spirit of God dwells in you?" The miracle working power of God lives in you, this power has made residence IN you. Christ in YOU the living hope of Glory. This is a permanent residency, not temporary! In the first definition of dynamis it also states "inherent power." Inherent by standard dictionary terms means: existing in someone or something as a permanent and inseparable element. Glory to God! NOTHING can separate you from the miracle working power of God that lives and abides in you, and that is just the first definition of dynamis we have covered. According to the second definition, it is the power to perform miracles! It just keeps getting better! Jesus said,

**"Most assuredly, I say to you, he who be-
lieves in Me, the works that I do he will do
also; and GREATER works than these he will
do, because I go to My Father."
John 14:12 NKJV**

Jesus really releases a key here to your authority and power working "effectively." Again, one can have authority and power and not exercise it. Jesus here states it is "he who believes in Me."

This does not only mean believing Jesus is alive, but that Jesus is the Word. *"And the Word became flesh..." John 1:14.* We must believe in the Word of God and WHO the Word says we are. Those who do not believe they have authority and miracle working power, will see little results in their life, families and realm of influence. Just because you experience resistance to your authority at times, does not mean that you have not been given full authority and power. Do you really think the devil is just going to "bend over" and go the extra mile for you? He will resist arrest! Although he may resist arrest, as you pull out your gun like an officer of the law, and pull the trigger on that miracle working power he will have to obey. When you pull out your hand cuffs and bind the devil with your words, he will be bound.

"And I will give you the keys of the Kingdom of Heaven. Whatever you forbid on earth will be forbidden in heaven, and whatever you permit on earth will be permitted in heaven."
Matthew 16:19 NLT

There it is! The keys! Glory to God! You do not give someone who has no authority keys! We choose what to allow and not allow on earth and heaven! Wow! Whatever you have the keys to is your realm and influence of authority. If you have keys to a house...that house is under your jurisdiction and authority. You go through the door with the keys to the house, not the window! Only a thief goes through the window, or someone with no authority. If someone comes through the window of your house, and grabs your computer system, and starts to walk out the door with it, you don't just sit there and let them walk out do you? No! You exercise your authority and you tell that popper to put the computer back and if they resist then you have them arrested. Just as it would be insane to allow a thief to come into your house illegally, so it is for us not to forbid sickness and disease in our life or anything that is sub-standard to the promises of God for our life. We have the right and authority to forbid anything from touching us that is not of God, and we have the right to allow and give it permission to remain. Anything we see in our lives that is good or bad is there by permission. If you see the devil stealing anything in your life, you have the right to tell him to "PUT IT BACK"!   Smith Wigglesworth, who played a major role in the move of God in the early 1900's in the miraculous things of God, had an encounter with the devil himself. Wigglesworth was sleeping one night when the devil came to pay him a visit. The devil thought he would scare him and began to move his bed across the room. In my mind, I imagine this incident as the devil being very dramatic... a dark cloud coming in, and a "eerie" and cold presence probably filled the room... then the bed starts moving across the room. Wigglesworth wakes up, and realizes his bed is moving while he is in it! Wigglesworth knowing his authority, sits up in bed and says to the devil with authority, "Put it back!" And the devil moves the bed back right where he got it from! Isn't that like the devil to make everything so dramatic? Don't pay any attention to the drama that the devil or the world throws at you. It's no different in this life we live in now. In this life Jesus promised us that there will be trials and tribulations, however, thank God we have victory over them all because of the authority that's been given unto us. We must exercise our authority, and we must believe in the power of God that lives in us. If the devil is trying to steal anything, you tell him to PUT IT BACK! It is your right, privilege and authority to tell the devil what to do and where to go!

Chapter Five

The Highest Authority

For us to understand the authority that has been given us, we must recognize the highest authority. The absolute highest authority in heaven and earth is the Word of the living God. There is no other that is higher. The Word of God is the highest authority because the Word of God IS God; God pre-existed before anything or anyone.

"In the beginning was the Word, and the Word was with God and the Word was God."
John 1:1 NKJV

The Word of God is the highest authority. What the Word of God says-goes. What the Word of God says-is the final word on the matter. God spoke the worlds into existence. The Word of God carries within itself the very essence and nature and integrity of the word that is being spoken. When God said, "Let there be light" – a potato didn't show up! The integrity of the Word is "light." Within the word spoken in it, was "light." Whatever God speaks is the ultimate final word and say so. Have you ever seen a child test a parent? The child asks the parent for something, and the parent says "no". Then the child goes away for a while...then comes back and asks the same question again, and the answer is the same, the parent says, "no." Then the child asks, "Why?", and the parent responds... "Because I said so." The child proceeds to ask again...and again... finally the parent gets to the point of frustration and possibly a bit angry and says, "I said, NO! And that is the final word!" This is the way our enemy is... he persists over and over again, poking you in your thought life, trying to get you to look at the world in recession, trying to get you to look at your bills, and get you to say "I just can't get ahead financially." He will continue to try to break into your word and steal the Word of God from you that says, "You are rich." When the devil comes at you and says you are poor you have to come back and say, "No! I am rich because the Word of God says, "Jesus became poor so I can be RICH! And that is the final word!" You do that by your words and your actions in making the Word of God the final say so, because it is the highest authority. When the devil comes at you to say that you are "running out" that you are in "lack" – you have the right and the authority to GIVE, and sow a seed! That is the time to exercise your authority. Don't let the devil tell you what to do with your checkbook when it comes to giving to God! You have every right to give to God. Exercise your authority on the word, *"Give and it shall be given unto you, good measure, pressed down, shaken together and running over will be put into your bosom. For with the measure you use, it will be measured back to you." Luke 6:38* When God spoke the sun into existence it is under the highest authority and it rises and goes down at the Word of God. It shines and radiates at the Word of the living God. The Word of God gives the command to the elements of the earth and what they are to do. By the Word of God the universes exist, by the Word of God, we have seasons of summer, fall, winter, and spring. By the Word of God the trees lose their leaves during fall and gain them back in spring. By the Word of God the earth rotates around the sun. By the Word of God the moon shines at night. Even the elements, and the universe recognize the highest authority and obey Him. What do you think will happen when you recognize the Word of God as the highest authority?

We have that same miracle working breath of

God living in us, Christ. When we speak our words are carrying the essence, ability and integrity of that word. When things come and oppose us, and try to get us to agree out of our mouth with them, we must combat it, by coming back and making the decision that God's Word is THE final word on the subject, and reject all others. This is where we fight the good fight of faith and WIN!

There are no "maybes", "hoping" or "wishing" in God's Word. The Word of God must be the final "say so" in every circumstance and aspect in and of your life. The word of God doesn't say, "All who call on the name of the Lord "might" be saved." The word does not say, "just a few who call on the Lord shall be saved." No! It says, *"For whoever calls on the name of the Lord shall be saved." Romans 10:13 NKJV* That word "saved" in the Greek is "sozo" which means; to keep safe, to rescue from danger and destruction, to save from suffering, from disease, to make well, to heal, to deliver, to save from the evils which obstruct the reception of the Messiah. This means it is your right to be walking in healing, deliverance, and anything that gets in the way of Gods will for your life and the promises of God. If any of this is being jeopardized, then you have the right to sentence and judge that thing. When you believe the Word, and take what the Word says over your life instead of what the world is throwing at you, and life's ups and downs, it's then that the Word of God can move in your life. You must submit to what the Word of God says about you. When the Word of God says you are healed, then for you to say you are "sick" is out of agreement with God's word, and you have re-aligned yourself with another authority that is not of God. For a Believer to say they are "poor" is like a millionaire saying he is "impoverished" in the monetary realm. It's not correct. When we declare and decide to accept what the world circumstances are saying about us then we have voided our authority in those areas of our life, as we have chosen to believe in the integrity of the circumstance, instead of the integrity of the Word of God. On the other hand, when we rise up, and we say, "NO" to those things which are opposing us, and opposing the word of God, our authority becomes active and effective.

Chapter Six

Citizens of a New Kingdom

It is important to understand that we do not have this authority on our own accord, or our works. Just as we cannot earn salvation, we cannot earn authority. Authority is a part of salvation. Once born again, we are immediately transferred from the kingdom of darkness to the kingdom of light. This makes us citizens of a different kingdom, different than the rest of the world. Citizens have rights. If you are an American citizen or a citizen of any country, that country gives you rights. You are now born of God's kingdom and you have rights according to His Kingdom. In order to access these rights you must exercise your God given authority. This authority has been given or "delegated" to us, by Jesus and His act of obedience to the cross. By connection of believing His Word and not being separated from God we now have access to this authority. Although we now have access to this great and amazing authority, we must also understand that we are still UNDER authority. No one is ever exempt from being under authority. Everyone whether a Believer or un-believer is under some sort of authority. It doesn't even matter if you believe in authority, every person under the sun is under some sort of rule. Unbelievers are under the devils authority. According to the Word our father is the devil until we are born again.

"You are of your father the devil..."
John 8:44 NKJV

Believers are in the Kingdom of light, they can choose to be under the wrong authority and not even know it. The Word says, "My people perish for a lack of knowledge." Thus it is extremely important to understand how authority works!

Just as the Word of God is the highest authority in heaven, earth and under the earth, so is the name of Jesus. *"And the Word became flesh..." John 1:14 NKJV* The Word and Jesus are One. Jesus is The Word. This makes His name of the highest authority. We cannot separate Jesus from the Word.

Jesus said, "And these signs will follow those who believe: In My name they will cast out demons; they will speak with new tongues; they will take up serpents; and if they drink anything deadly it will by no means hurt them; they will lay hands on the sick and they will recover."
Mark 16:17

In the above verse we are also provided, as Believers, with power to cast out devils, we are given the power to pray in an angelic language that will bring results in heaven and earth, and are kept safe and protected from anything that might try to bring harm, as being provided with the ability to see others healed. The name of Jesus provides authority for us and extends to all those around us who may need help.

In My name means: "the name is used for everything which the name covers, it is used for ones rank, authority, interests, commands, and deeds." When we are using the name of Jesus, it is used for everything that Jesus has covered, as He said, *"All authority has been given unto Me in heaven and Earth."* When using His name every-thing is covered and we have the legal right to use it to see people healed, to reject those things that would try to harm us, and to cast out any devil that is trying to take our territory, whether it is a territory of physical health, finances, peace, or joy. We have been given the rank of His authority, which He carries to be able to carry out and enforce His will on this earth. *Psalms 119:89 says, "Forever O Lord, Your word is settled in heaven."* We do not need this authority in heaven! His word is already established in heaven, but due to law breakers down here on earth, it is our duty as Believers to receive the rank of Christ, and enforce His will here on earth. Some of you reading this just cringed when you read "*receive the rank of Christ.*" Does that put you on His level? Are we blaspheming here? No! We most certainly are not deity as Christ is, but we have been given the same position in heavenly places as Christ.

"and raised us up together, and made us sit together in the heavenly places in Christ Jesus."
Ephesians 2:6

We were raised with Christ when He rose from the dead. When we gave our life to Him we became a new creation, and now Christ is IN us as per Colossians 1:27 "...*Christ IN you the hope of Glory.*" This means Christ is in us, and we are in Him. That

46

puts us right with Him at the right hand of God. We are in the greatest seat of authority that oversees the universes. Wow!

Chapter Seven

A Strong Tower

"The name of the Lord is a strong tower; the righteous man runs into it and is safe."
Proverbs 18:10

What is really in a name? Have you heard of name droppers? They are people that mention names of important and influential people to gain recognition or a higher place of favor. In the world who you associate with reflects the amount of influence and power that backs you up. If you are a person who associates with a group of billionaires people would look at you and say, "ok, let's do what they say, as they have the power to back up what they are saying because of who they associate with." Yet if a person associates with a group of people who work at McDonalds, flipping burgers, and frying french fries...and that person says, "I'm going to build a three billion dollar skyscraper." People would not respond to that person or even take seriously what they said, as they do not have the power to back up what they are saying.

"Therefore God also has highly exalted Him and given Him the name which is above every name, that at the name of Jesus every knee should bow, of those in heaven, and of those on the earth and those under the earth."
Philippians 2:9-10

Here we see that the name of Jesus is above every name in heaven, earth and under the earth. Why the name? When we understand that everything has a name, then we understand we have authority over EVERYTHING! God gave mankind the power to name anything and everything in the earth from the beginning. He had Adam naming the animals and mankind is still doing the same thing today. We discover something and give it a "name" to identify it and its characteristics. What does the medical community give to symptoms they discover in peoples bodies? They give it a name! Cancer is just a name folks. Diabetes is just a name. Fibromyalgia is a name. High blood pressure is a name. HIV is a name. All these physical ailments/diseases are just names. They carry within them certain physical characteristics, but all these things are subject to the name of Jesus. The name that is above every name. Just as everything has a name, everything has ears! When you speak to the name of cancer, when you speak to the name of diabetes, they have ears to hear what you are saying and when you come in the name of Jesus, they must submit and obey. Just as the name of cancer carries in the characteristics of physical symptoms, the name of Jesus carries all the characteristics of the power of the resurrection. This means the name of Jesus carries the destructive force to _crush_ all that opposes His word. It carries the power to save a person from hell and it carries the power to rescue us out of destruction, it carries the power to mend a broken bone, it carries the power to destroy a tumor, it carries the power to forgive, to heal, to protect, and to make new. The name of Jesus can create a new kidney, and can even put a $1000 in your bank account if you need it!

Have you ever seen someone in an intense circumstance that is pressuring them and what they do? Even if they are not Believers, they call on the name of Jesus! Someone in a life or death situation,

automatically out of their spirit they cry out "Jesus!"
Even if that person is a Buddhist or Muslim! In the
most intensified situation they will cry out "Jesus!"
God has instilled a consciousness in humankind of
His existence. Whether they acknowledge it or not,
they know. You will even find an atheist crying out
the name of Jesus when they are in a life or death
situation!

God has given us Jesus' name so that we can
have His kind of results. Not just the results Jesus
had on earth, but the results He has even now!

**"Love has been perfected among us in this:
that we may have boldness in the day of
judgment; because <u>as He is,
so are we in this world.</u>"
1 John 4:17 NKJV**

Just as Christ is NOW, so are we in this world is
what 1st John 4:17 is telling us. The Word is the
ultimate authority. We must receive this word that
we are just like Christ in this world. To act on this
word all we have to do is receive and believe it!
Everything we do must be done in His name to get
His results. When we do things in our own name,
we will only get our results which are works of the
flesh. Our name will get us very little and

limited results. We need the name of Jesus to enforce God's Kingdom, which we are citizens of when we become born again. It's because of His name that we do not have to be "moved" when things rise against us. We have the name that has all power and authority backing us up. The battles we fight in life, the good fight of faith are all over names and words.

"The name of the Lord is a strong tower; the righteous man runs into it and is safe." Proverbs 18:10

I love this verse! The name of the Lord is a strong tower! A tower is a high place. The person that has the high ground on the battlefield is ALWAYS the one who has the advantage. We being seated in heavenly places gives us that high ground that we need to be victorious in every situation, which we do by exercising His name. A tower is also a safe place of protection and sanctuary, as it is a place that is literally unreachable by the enemy's artillery. When you are in that secret place of the heavenly position, the enemy's fiery darts may be shot UP at you but will never reach you! It takes faith to know you have the right and authority to sit in heavenly places at the right hand of God, right alongside with Jesus.

A tower is never alone. It is always accompanied by a castle! Castles began to be built in 900 AD and they weren't much to look at. The first castles were built with dirt and timber and they did not have towers at this time. As the structure progressed in the twelfth and thirteenth centuries they began building castles with stones instead of dirt and timber. They built gigantic walls. These walls would be up to ten feet thick and thirty-nine feet high! They were built with the purpose to defend a country and dominate the population. It was in these centuries that Christian crusaders, realized their current design was being breached and came up with a divine idea which was surely from heaven, the tower. This new architecture accelerated them from being a victim to a structure of victory. Due to the new development they were now able to maximize their fire power with the flanking fire that they would throw off the walls of the tower. The towers would act as a guide for the artillery to funnel down and hit its target.

Just as castles were originally built with dirt and things of the earth so was the first man, Adam. The tower came later and fortified mankind, the second heavenly man, is Jesus.

"The first name was of the earth, made of

dust; the second Man is the Lord from heaven." 1st Corinthians 15:47

The first name was of the earth. The first name was Adam, and we got Adams results! The second name was Jesus. With the name of Jesus we now have access to heavenly results.

When Jesus came we went from earthy to living stones, and we bare the heavenly image of Him. Jesus is the chief corner stone and we are the living stones.

"Coming to Him as to a living stone, rejected indeed by men, but chosen by God and precious, you also as living stones, are being built up a spiritual house, a holy priesthood, to offer up spiritual sacrifices acceptable to God through Jesus Christ. Therefore it is also contained in the Scripture, 'Behold, I lay in Zion A chief cornerstone, elect, precious, And he who believes on Him will by no means be put to shame." 1st Peter 2:4-6

"But you are a chosen generation, a royal priesthood, a holy nation, His own special people, that you may proclaim the praises of Him who called you out of darkness into His marvelous light; who once were not a people but are now the people of God, who had not

obtained mercy but now have obtained mercy." 1st Peter 2:9-10

Together, all the lively stones, and with Christ we make up The Church. We are members of His body, and citizens of His Kingdom. If we are His body, surely His name that is a strong tower is our name also. Our name to use, and from a high heavenly place, where we can see things a far off, and know that any weapon formed against us is not going to prosper, and surely not going to hit the tower! It is impossible for the Tower to take a "hit", if Christ's name is the Strong Tower. Christ defeated the devil, defeated death and the grave, He doesn't take hits, He gives them!

The name of the LORD is a strong tower; the righteous man runs into it and is safe.
Proverbs 18:10 ESV

I want to bring attention to "a righteous man runs into it..." It is not "run in to it" as if you ran into a brick wall and bumped your head. It is run into as if you are "inside" something. We are _in_ the tower. This is where we live! This is where we move and have our being. This is where we are to abide in. The towers had many levels. When the tower was not needed for military purposes, the servants used the interior levels for living quarters. If we live in the tower, our shield of faith must be up and active, as it is the shield of faith that quenches all the fiery darts. If we are in the tower, that is made of stone, built on the chief cornerstone, if we are in Christ, and He is in us, how can anything harm us? If God be for us, who can be against us? We are surrounded by Glory!

"You crown the year with Your goodness,
And Your paths drip with abundance."
Psalms 65:11 NKJV

In the above verse, "crown" means to "encircle" or "surround for attack." Goodness is God's glory. Your year has been marked with God's glory and your year is surrounded by His goodness! You are surrounded by Him.   His name is a strong tower that surrounds you with the thick walls of Glory.

His name is protection and a refuge, but it is also for action. Jesus said, "*And these signs will follow those who believe: In My name they will cast out demons; they will speak with new tongues; they will take up serpents; and if they drink anything deadly, it will by no means hurt them; they will lay hands on the sick, and they will recover." Mark 16:17-18*
In His name alone, we have the ability to cast out

devils, speak in a heavenly language, heal the sick. And if anything comes at us to try to harm us, it will not because we are in Him. His name covers both defense and offense. His name covers everything!

This is also delegated authority. We see Jesus in *Mark 16* sending us with His name. He has delegated out His authority for us to occupy this planet with it. If you are an employer and you delegate one of your employees to take care of a task for you, you expect that employee to carry out the task given. The employer will also give the employee the supplies and equipment needed to get the task done. If anyone should confront or oppose the employee while trying to accomplish the task, that employee has every right to say, "My employer has given me the power and authority to carry out this task." It is the same with the name of Jesus. You have been given the authority to cast out any devil that is opposing the call of God on your life and opposing God's best for you. Jesus has sent you with His authority to carry out His will. His will is His Word. He expects us to operate in His authority under His name and has given us the equipment and divine ability we need to get the job done! God doesn't send us on a mission and not give us the ability to fulfill that mission. *He has given us everything that pertains to life and godliness according to 2nd Peter 1:3.*

Just as you never see a tower by itself, it is always attached to a castle, so are we never alone when we live and have our being in Christ and allow the name of the Lord to be that strong tower for us. All we have to do is accept this word as Truth, making a decision to allow this Word to be the ultimate authority in our life, that His name is ours, His name is a safe place of protection and refuge, as well as a name to use on the offensive if the devil tries to take anything from you, or put something on you.

It does not matter what you are facing right now. When you can look at your circumstance as words and names then you know you have come to the understanding of the authority that has been given to you, seated in heavenly places at the right hand of God. A person who sits there most certainly has the right and rank to command and decree things and they will obey. We command from the place of the Strong Tower with the name of Jesus!

As we have learned everything has a name, there is one exception to this. We do find one being who does not have a name. That entity is satan. In *Isaiah 14:12 "How art thou fallen from heaven, O Lucifer.." NKJ. We find later that Jesus said, "I beheld satan as lightning fall from heaven."*

NKJV Why did Isaiah say Lucifer and Jesus said "satan?" Satan's name when he lived in heaven was Lucifer which meant: shining one, morning star. But when satan was quickly demoted and removed from heaven, he lost his name! He was no longer Lucifer. Satan is just a term to describe that we are talking about "the fallen one." Satan means "adversary." Satan really doesn't have a name because a name implies there is some sort of authority. Jesus defeated him on the cross so badly that He took satans keys that he had over hell, death and the earth, as well as disarmed him and made a public spectacle of him and all his buddies. (Col 2:15) He has been stripped of all authority and power. There is no safe tower for the adversary. He has no high ground and no advantage. We have the privilege of exercising the name that is above all names in heaven, earth and under the earth! Glory! We do not come in our own name anymore, as our name gets us our results, but we come in the name of Jesus, which gives us access to His results and no limits, as all things are possible through Christ Jesus.

We find in Acts 19 how the name of Jesus affects those who know of Jesus' name and those who know Jesus. Although the enemy has been stripped of his name, he does acknowledge names that are abiding in the strong tower.

A group of Jews was traveling from town to town casting out evil spirits. They tried to use the name of the Lord Jesus in their incantation, saying, *"I command you in the name of Jesus, whom Paul preaches, to come out!" Acts 19:13 NLT*

And the evil spirit answered and said, "Jesus I know, and Paul I know; but who are you?" Acts 19:15 NKJV

Not just anyone can use the name of Jesus. The Jewish exorcists tried using the name of Jesus but it just got them into trouble! The name of Jesus didn't work for them. When they tried using the name of Jesus to cast out an evil spirit, the unclean spirit answered back that it knew Jesus, and knew Paul. *The TCNT translation says, "Jesus I acknowledge, Paul I acknowledge..."* the devil won't acknowledge just anybody! The Jews knew <u>of</u> Jesus, and were trying to do the "name dropper" thing. You cannot "name drop" with the name of Jesus and get results. The only way to get results with the name of Jesus is to be qualified. To be qualified one must be born again, or born of the spirit. Jesus said, *"Most assuredly, I say to you, unless one is born of water and the Spirit, he cannot enter the kingdom of God".* If you are just born of water you will only get this natural realm results. The devil only acknowledges

61

a new creation in Christ Jesus, because he has no legal right or rule over the new creation.

Let's look at what happened before the account of the failed exorcism. We see Paul coming in contact with some of John the Baptists disciples in Acts 19:2-6 NKJV and questioning them about their baptism;

"Did you receive the Holy Spirit when you believed?" So they said to him, "We have not so much as heard whether there is a Holy Spirit."

And he said to them, "Into what then were you baptized?" So they said, "Into John's baptism."

Then Paul said, "John indeed baptized with a baptism of repentance, saying to the people that they should believe on Him who would come after him, that is, on Christ Jesus."

When they heard this, they were baptized in the **name of the Lord Jesus.**

And when Paul had laid hands on them, the Holy Spirit came upon them, and they spoke with tongues and prophesied.

We see from the above scriptures that Paul asks them if they had received the Holy Spirit yet, as John baptized unto repentance that they should believe on Him who would come after him, that is Christ Jesus. The word says that when these disciples heard this and believed in their heart they were instantly baptized in the name of the Lord Jesus, then Paul immediately laid hands on them and they received the baptism of the Holy Spirit and spoke in new tongues and prophesied. Up till this point those disciples were functioning in John the Baptist's name and had no power. They had an anointing for repentance, but no power demonstrations of Christ Jesus. It is only under the strong tower of the name of Jesus that there is power, protection and provision. *Philippians 2:9-10 says, "Therefore God also has highly exalted Him and given Him **the name which is above every name,** that at the name of Jesus every knee should bow, of those in heaven, and of those on earth, and of those under the earth.*

The name of Mary is not going to produce any power, the name of John the Baptist isn't going to produce any power. Not even the name of Elijah! It is the name of Jesus that positions us in a strong tower of power. The Jewish exorcists were clearly not inside the strong tower of the name of the Lord.

They had no right to use the name of Jesus as they were not born of the spirit, and the results were costly. They were beaten, stripped of their clothes and overcome by the darkness. When we are inside the strong tower of power, Jesus Christ, nothing can overcome you. Nothing can strip you and leave you naked. Nothing can beat you. No bills can overcome you. No disease can come upon you. No situation or circumstance can overtake you. No darkness can overcome you. The only thing that is capable of overtaking you, when inside the strong tower of the name of Jesus, is His goodness and His blessings!

"And all these blessings shall come upon you and overtake you, because you obey the voice of the Lord your God."
Deuteronomy 28:2 NKJV

Deuteronomy goes on to list all the blessings that shall overtake a person who is living and abiding in the strong tower by obeying His voice. His voice is His Word. The list goes on and on of the blessings that the Lord has for you that will come upon and overtake you. From being blessed in the city, to blessed in the country. That covers you everywhere you go! You can safely say I am blessed no matter where you are! Even in the midst of the most trying circumstances you can say, "I am blessed!".

Lets take a look at the rest of the blessings that are appointed to overtake those who live and abide in the strong tower:

Vs. 4 - ""Blessed shall be the fruit of your body, the produce of your ground and the increase of your herds, the increase of your cattle and the offspring of your flocks."

Your children are blessed and everything that is under your stewardship that God has given you is blessed, and the offspring of harvest coming off of what has been given to you is also blessed. It's a perpetual blessing of multiplication that never stops!

Vs. 7 - "The Lord will cause your enemies who rise against you to be defeated before your face; they shall come out against you one way and flee before you seven ways."

Our enemy lurks around those whom he "may" devour. He may not devour one who is in the strong tower of His name. Those things that are not lined up with the Word in your life are anti-anointing, they will not be able to stay in the presence of a blessed man or woman of God.

Vs. 11-"And the Lord will grant you plenty of goods in the fruit of your body, in the increase of your live-

stock and in the product of your ground and in the land of which the Lord swore to your fathers to give you.

Vs. 12 – "The Lord will open to you His good treasure, the heavens, to give the rain to your land in its season, and to bless all the work of your hand. You shall lend to many nations, but you shall not borrow."

The Lord even opens His treasures of goodness from the heavens to you! Rain to bring increase and growth, and to bless everything your hand touches. He makes you a lender and not a borrower. He makes you the head and not the tail. He has made you rich with all these blessings.

The prerequisites for abiding in all these blessings are just simply to obey His Word, His commandments. It is the ones that that live in the strong tower of the name of Jesus that these blessings belong to, and everyone will see the blessing on your life! There is global attention even now that has turned its eyes upon The Church. Not just any church. The eyes of the world are not on the Muslim church, they are not on the New Age church, they are not on any church except The Body of Christ that makes up The Church.

*Vs. 9-10 - "The Lord will establish you as a holy people to Himself, just as He has sworn to you, if you keep the commandments of the Lord your God and walk in His ways. Then all peoples of the earth shall see that you are **called by the name of the Lord,** and they shall be afraid of you."*

Did we just read that right? All the people of the earth (global) will see those that are called by the name of the Lord and they shall be afraid of us. The name of the Lord is a strong tower and the righteous run in to it! It's no wonder the righteous run in to it, its no wonder the righteous live and move and have their being in the name of Jesus. The strong tower of the name of the Lord is protection and refuge of safety. We tend to think of protection as a "defense". In reality it is more than a defense, it's an offense. If a mother bear senses her cubs are in some sort of danger that mother bear is going to do everything in its power to be sure those cubs are safe, even if it means taking out an opposing force. If a mother bear is that protective over her cubs, how much more is our Father in Heaven and our big brother Jesus going to protect us? The strong tower Himself said: *"Do not think that I came to bring peace on earth. I did not come to bring peace but a sword.*

Matthew 10:24 NKJV

The sword is His word that can cut through the deepest marrow and joints, that can cut and tear down, as well as build up and heal. The sword of His word and anointing will literally destroy the yoke and obliterate it into pieces that cannot be mended.

Even after the failed exorcism, when people saw the Jews totally overpowered by the evil spirit in Acts 19, because they weren't born again, to be able to use the name of the Lord, there was great fear that fell among the people. Not fear of the devil, but fear of the power of God and the name of the Lord.

"This became known both to all Jews and Greeks dwelling in Ephesus; and fear fell on them all, and the_name of the Lord Jesus was magnified."
Acts 19:17

There is a reason the religious and political leaders were constantly telling the Apostles that they cannot minister in the name of Jesus. They were free to minister in any other name, but not the name of Jesus! They were afraid of the name. Thank God they didn't follow those orders! Even today, we see people offended by the name of Jesus because they are afraid of the power it carries. Look at the forces that have tried to take prayer out of schools. What are they after? They are after the name of Jesus. We even have seen Christian ministries back off the name of Jesus to "not" offend people. This cannot be. We must not hide the name of Jesus, but instead we must MAGNIFY the name of Jesus. If you cannot magify and preach the name of Jesus, then you have no business being in the ministry and you need to get saved. To push down the name of Jesus is purely anti-Christ. Do not pull back from the name that is above every other name in heaven and earth. If you fnd yourself in a situation that is pressuring you to not use the name of Jesus, know that it is only because they are afraid and are in fear.

The name of the Lord is a **strong tower,** and there is nothing that can overcome it. All darkness is terrified of this name, Jesus. This is the name you carry. This is the name that covers you. This is the name that protects and delivers you. This is the name that heals and defends you. This is the name that causes your enemies to flee seven ways. This is the name that causes multiplication to happen in your life. This is the name that has all authority in heaven, on earth and under the earth, and it belongs to you. This is what gives you the power and ability to be the overcomer instead of the one that is overcome. This is the victory that overcomes the world, even our faith, according to 1st John 4-5:

"Who is he who overcomes the world, but he who believes that Jesus is the Son of God?"

Jesus, is the name you live and abide in. This is the name where The Church abides, and is a great fortress. You are a part of greatness and power that cannot be overcome by any darkness or any anti-Christ kingdom. This is the strong tower of power that belongs to every child of God.

Chapter Eight

The Power of Being Under

My favorite example of delegated authority is the centurion that we find in Luke 7. We find that the centurion had a servant that he loved dearly, who was sick and dreadfully tormented, ready to die the Word says. That is about as sick as you can get! The centurion sends word to Jesus to come and "heal" his servant. You will notice the centurion did not ask Jesus to come and "pray" for him that his servant "might" be healed. In verse 6 of chapter 7 we find Jesus not far from the servant's house when He is met by the centurion's friends who deliver a message to Jesus. The message says:

"Lord, do not trouble Yourself, for I am not worthy that You should enter under my roof. (Verse 7) Therefore I did not even think myself worthy to come to You. But say the word, and my servant will be healed."

Somewhere between verse 3 and verse 6 the centurion received a revelation of authority! As in verse 3 he had his friends pleading for Jesus to come and heal. In verse 6 and 7 the centurion is saying, "Hey, I am not worthy for <u>YOU</u> to be <u>UNDER</u> my roof." What does that mean? The centurion being a soldier himself grasped the meaning of authority and that Jesus' authority was greater than his, and he is not worthy for that kind of a high authority to be *UNDER* his command. The centurion recognized that the correct order of authority is for him to be *UNDER* the Word's authority and not the other way around. Then the centurion even goes further and he says, *"Just say the word and my servant will be healed."* Again the centurion is recognizing the highest authority in the heavens and earth, and that the Word of God is living and carries in it the integrity and power of substance of the Word itself. The centurion was so sure of the Word that Jesus would speak and that it would heal his servant that there was no need for Jesus to come. He had decided the Word would be the <u>*ultimate authority*</u> in this circumstance. Most people want the minister to come to their house. We see clearly that the centurion has received this revelation when he says in verse 8; "For I also am a man placed *under authority*, having soldiers under me. And I say to one, 'Go' and he goes; and to another, 'Come,' and he comes; and to my servant, 'Do this,' and he does it."

The centurion recognized the highest authority and understood that he himself is UNDER that authority and that even though he is under authority, he also has others that are "under" him whom he can command what to do and where to go. We call this the "chain of command." This is where we need to be, Believer! Recognize we are under the highest authority, the Word of God, and yet there are things that are "under" us that we can command to go and come. What is under you? ALL THINGS! Yes, all things are under you. The earth is the Lords.
Jesus paid the price for us to once again have dominion and authority over the earth. This means even the elements of the earth are under you and will respond to you, when you know your authority.

"And He put all things under His feet, and gave Him to be head over ALL THINGS to the church, which is His body, the fullness of Him who fills all in all."
Ephesians 1:22-23 NKJV

Everything is under Jesus' feet, and we being the body of Christ means that all things are UNDER us. If the earth is under us, surely our circumstances are under us, surely our bills are under us, surely sickness and disease are under us, surely poverty is under us, surely according to the highest authority, every devil is subject to us! Glory!

The centurion recognized that these things are under him and that he has the right and jurisdiction to command them to "come" or "go." Believer, if you need something to come to you, then command it to come and if there is something that needs to LEAVE your life, tell it where it can go! I can definitely think of some good places to send some devils.

We see in verse 9 of chapter 7 of Luke that Jesus marveled at the centurion and said, "I say to you, I have not found such great faith, not even in Israel." This tells us that great faith and authority are connected. Great faith is the realm of the miraculous! This is the power that backs up the authority. When you make the Word of God the ultimate authority and the final word in your life is when you see heaven move in the miraculous!

"For sin will have NO dominion over you,
since you are not under
law but under grace."
Romans 6:14 RSV

No longer is your father the devil. No longer is sin over you, but UNDER you. You are now under grace, which means favor, divine ability and God's influence. You are under God's influence, not sins influence! If you are being influenced by something other than God and His Word... then you have the right and authority to tell that thing to get UNDER your feet, and rise above it. All you have to do Believer is receive the Word of God, believe it and act on it, believe that you are over and not under. The only thing you are under is God's Word. I wouldn't want to be under anything else!

Every day we have a choice of what authority we are under. Every time we choose to agree and believe God's Word then we are UNDER His authority and able to operate in our delegated authority as Believers. Every time we choose to believe a circumstance or a symptom that is not lining up with God's Word we have just positioned ourselves under that lying authority. Whatever we are believing is what we are subject to. Whatever we are believing is the authority we are under. If we choose to position ourselves under a circumstance or lying symptoms authority, we are choosing that rule over The Truth, over God's Word. We then have forfeited our Heavenly dominion and the delegated authority that was given to us no longer works. In order to get back into the heavenly, delegated authority realm, all we must do is repent by changing our minds to believe God's Word as the final word and "say so." God's Word is the <u>ULTIMATE AUTHORITY</u> not just in this earth, but in the UNIVERSE! God's Word never returns void. Although His Word is the ultimate authority, we can position ourselves under a different authority by the daily decisions we make. We are all under authority - it is just a matter of which kingdom you are going to believe? Are you going to believe in the integrity of the world? Are you going to believe in the integrity of the circumstance? Or are you going to believe in the integrity of the Word of God and what it has to say about your life?

Chapter Nine

Harnessing The Power

In Matthew 17:14-21 we find that the disciples could not cast out the devil of an epileptic boy. The disciples had cast out devils with no issues up to this point. This wasn't their first devil that they had run into. We see in chapter 10 of Matthew that Jesus sent the disciples out in His authority, then Jesus commanded them in verse 8 to "heal the sick, cleanse the lepers, raise the dead, cast out demons. Freely you have received, freely give." Then when the disciples came back from their mission trips in Luke 10:17 they reported back, *"Lord even the demons are subject to us in Your Name."* It is very clear that the disciples were already familiar with exercising their exousia and casting out devils. So what happened with the epileptic boy? Authority is not always enough by itself. You must be able to harness the dynamis power of God. Remember dynamis is the miracle working power of God. You can do a lot with just the authority of the name of Jesus. His name is above every name. There comes a time when you need the miracle working power to back up and perform the will of God. Jesus literally busted the disciples on two factors they were lacking with this particular demoniac, faith and dynamis. Jesus informed the disciples that they were unable to cast this demon out due to unbelief or "lack of faith" and proceeded to say "however this kind does not go out except by prayer and fasting." Jesus was saying your faith level is not where it should be AND you have not spent time in prayer and fasting. Faith comes by hearing. No matter what you are hearing will affect your faith level. If your authority is not working check to see who you are hanging around listening to. Are you listening more to the news and the world crises on CNN than you are spending time with God? Are you hanging around people who speak doubt and unbelief? What are your ears plugged into? Into the Word of God or the world? These things will short circuit your authority and power.

Prayer hooks you directly into the power of God. Fasting puts you on the fast track in acquiring answers and performance as you seek God. Studying the Word will bring faith, because faith comes by hearing of the Word. Although studying the Word of God is very necessary, studying in itself is not going to bring you power. It brings faith. Faith is the doorway to the power of God if you act on it. Without faith it is impossible to please God. God cannot move on doubt and unbelief. He can only move on faith. It will lead you to the power, and bring your faith level up to step into the power of God with boldness. Fasting and prayer draws us near to God, who is our source of the power.

We are to be filled with faith and the Holy Ghost. When we get into the realm of prayer, we get closer to God and hear the Word of God. We cannot live on yesterday's manna, we have authority every day of the week, but you do not have anointing every day of the week unless you approach God that day to be anointed with fresh oil. We are never separated from the power of God, but we must harness the power of God by spending time in His presence and receiving from Him. If we try to work off the word from yesterday, and didn't take the time to draw near then the anointing we experienced yesterday can't help us today. There are mountains we face that need more than just authority but require the dynamis power of the living God to blast that thing out of the way. In order to be ready in season and out of season, we need to stay filled with the Spirit of God.   Pray! Pray in tongues, pray in English, but pray and commune with your Heavenly Father, and receive and replenish in His presence. If you find that you do not have time to pray some days you still can walk in the spirit. Just yield your spirit to Him, and keep Him on your mindset. Pray in your spirit. Your spirit can pray "always" according to the Apostle Paul in Ephesians 6:18. It's the connection to God!

In Isaiah 45:11 we find the Lord telling us to command Him!

"Thus says the Lord, The Holy One of Israel and his Maker: 'Ask Me of things to come concerning My sons; and concerning the word of My hands, YOU COMMAND ME.'"
Isaiah 45:11 NKJV

God wants us to command with authority His works. God wants us to command His promises for our lives. It is our right to command the hand of God to do His works. He does not want us to go in wimpily to the throne room in our time of need. He did not say to beg or ask Him to "someday" perform His word. He has given us the authority to command and speak things into existence. He is expecting us to command!

**"...God who gives life to the dead and calls
those things which do not exist
as though they did."
Romans 4:17 NKJV**

The promises of God give us the legal right to command. However we still need the dynamis power to carry out the command. Everyone who hears the promises of God has the right to participate and partake of what they are hearing. Unless we harness the dynamis power to see those promises carried out, it will sit there stagnant.

When you hook into the anointing you hook into what will answer all those things that oppose your body, that oppose your finances, that oppose the promises of God. Just like the woman with the issue of blood did in Mark 5:25. In the beginning she walked in the flesh and did everything in the natural. She went to every natural resource before she went to God. That was due to the fact that she had not "heard" yet of the healer. She was plugged into all the words of unbelief from the doctors and their reports of her condition. She believed at the time of the integrity of the doctors report. However, when she heard that there was a healer in town, she began to put her expectation (faith) on a different report than the doctors! She didn't waste any time in pressing into His presence to even just get a glimpse of Him. She sought Jesus out. She was pressing into the dynamis power of God. And when she pressed in and reached out she said in her heart, "If only I may touch His clothes, I shall be made well." She didn't say in her heart, "If I may touch his clothes 'maybe' I'll be healed." She didn't say in her heart, "if it be the Lords will" – she had tapped into her delegated right to be healed. She had the authority to command the blessing. By her authority she was able to harness the power of God right into her body!

WE HAVE THE AUTHORITY TO SAY I AM HEALED BY HIS STRIPES, ACCORDING TO ISAIAH 53! It is our right. By the blood poured out on the cross and the price paid, we have the right to say, "I am healed." We have the right to say, "pain be gone from my body." We have the right to say, "Jesus became poor so I can be rich, poverty get off me!" Your authority will always lead you to the miracle working power. The power of God will give you the break through needed. The devil always comes to steal, kill and destroy. He would like to steal your miracle. If you find that it appears that your miracle from God isn't working, it is just a façade. It is not the Truth. This is when you go right back to the Word, and even though it seems like something isn't working, the Word always works and never returns void. You must put the highest authority on it, The Word of God! Do not let the devil pull the wool over you eyes! Jesus came to give us life and life more abundantly. We cannot be unaware of the enemies schemes.

As we learn our authority and gain revelation of our authority we grow in it. God works in measures.

"But he who received the seed on good ground is he who hears the word and understands it, who indeed bears fruit and produces: some a hundred fold, some sixty some thirty."
Matthew 13:23 NKJV

All 3 examples of 100 fold, 60 fold, 30 fold, heard and understood the word. They are all good ground. Some were obviously on different levels of their understanding. When you first start learning your authority you want to go out and raise the dead! However you may be working on headache level authority. This is where people come back and say, "It doesn't work." This is not true. The Word of God works! If you ever find yourself saying "It doesn't work" the problem is never God or His Word. The problem is always us. Go back to the Word of God and find out what you are missing in your training. Start with taking authority in your immediate realm of influence, and grow from there. Remember a UFC fighter, in the natural, didn't just wake up one day and decide to step into the ring. They take months and years of training and equipping, fine tuning their technique and skills. It would be absurd for them to step into the ring with no training. If they did step into the ring with no training or conditioning they would inevitably lose that fight. How absurd would it be for that UFC fighter to be shocked that his opponent threw a punch to his face? Even more so, how absurd would it be for that UFC fighter not to throw back a punch and just sit there and let his opponent "wail" on him with blow after blow? How absurd would it be to blame their coach that they lost, when they didn't do what the coach told them to do? All these things seem ridiculous to us, yet it isn't that far off of an analogy of a Christian who is not taking training in the Word and Spirit of God seriously. They are shocked when a blow from the enemy comes, and then right after that blow, come several other blows, and they just sit there and take it! Then they blame the coach, which would be God or the Word of God. Here the Christian has been given authority over all of the enemies' power, as we have learned, but has had no training in it. It is the same when we say "it doesn't work", and it is an insult to God. You are saying "God doesn't work!". A true Ultimate Fighting Christian will not overlook their training in authority and dynamis power of God.

Do not assume because you get resistance that your authority isn't working. Remember the devil is a law breaker and he will push back as much as you will allow him. You give things permission to be or not to be.

You are created to walk in authority with power in order to receive the same results as Jesus does. This is what the devil is terrified of! He is terrified of authority. He not terrified of the Christian who just goes to church out of tradition and has no desire to grow in God. It is not you the devil is terrified of. It is Christ IN you that he is terrified of. By ourselves we do not have anything that impresses the devil. When we receive Christ and learn who we are in Him, and learn our authority, is when the devil begins to tremble and shake in terror. You, Believer are the greatest threat to the devil. Recognize the law breaker in your life, and begin to judge those things with your words. Declare God's promises in your life that belong to you and do not back off of the integrity of the Word of God. Make a decision for the Word of God to be the ultimate authority in your life.Recognizing that you are seated over all in heavenly places with Jesus Christ, and are under His Word, ruling and reigning in this life. This is what makes you the Ultimate Fighting Christian! Do not allow anything to tell you differently. You are created to walk in dominion, authority and power. Believer, now walk in it! Live in that strong tower of the name of Jesus Christ that has been provided for you!

Find M.D. Magruder-Krinock in your area,
visit:
www.mariakrinock.com

To schedule a ministry engagement
please contact us at:
contact@lifelineoutreach.com

NOTES:

NOTES:

NOTES:

NOTES:

NOTES:

_____

_____

_____

_____

_____

_____

_____

_____

_____

_____

_____

_____

_____

_____

_____

_____

_____

_____

_____

_____

_____

_____

NOTES:

NOTES:

_____
_____
_____
_____
_____
_____
_____
_____
_____
_____
_____
_____
_____
_____
_____
_____
_____
_____
_____
_____
_____
_____
_____
_____
_____
_____

NOTES:

_____
_____
_____
_____
_____
_____
_____
_____
_____
_____
_____
_____
_____
_____
_____
_____
_____
_____
_____
_____
_____
_____
_____

NOTES:

NOTES:

NOTES:

NOTES:

NOTES:

NOTES:

NOTES:

NOTES:

NOTES:

_____
_____
_____
_____
_____
_____
_____
_____
_____
_____
_____
_____
_____
_____
_____
_____
_____
_____
_____
_____
_____
_____
_____
_____

NOTES:

NOTES:

NOTES:

NOTES:

_____
_____
_____
_____
_____
_____
_____
_____
_____
_____
_____
_____
_____
_____
_____
_____
_____
_____
_____
_____
_____
_____
_____
_____
_____